Field Guide
to Forgiveness

poems by

Rebecca Watkins

Finishing Line Press
Georgetown, Kentucky

Field Guide
to Forgiveness

ACKNOWLEDGMENTS

Thank you to Juan Mobili for his invaluable feedback and guidance.

Thank you to the following publications and events in which these poems or
versions of them first appeared:

"Planning for the End of the World" *The BeZine*
"That Boy" and "Possibly Love" *Anti-Heroin Chic*
"The Long Drive" and "The Day I Heard" *New Feathers Anthology*
"After Some Time" *Nyack Poetry Walk*
"Embrace" Gallery & Reading for Poets Respond to Art, Arts Mid-Hudson
Organization

Publisher: Leah Huete de Maines
Editor: Christen Kincaid
Cover Art: Carolyn Watkins
Author Photo: Nina Skowronski
Cover Design: Elizabeth Maines McCleavy

Order online: www.finishinglinepress.com
                also available on amazon.com

Author inquiries and mail orders:
Finishing Line Press
PO Box 1626
Georgetown, Kentucky 40324
USA

Table of Contents

To my parents,
who taught me how to love and forgive.
To my husband,
who has loved me through storms.
To my stepdaughters,
who showed me that the hardest journeys
lead to the sweetest love.

blood & dreams

What Did I Know?

What can a daughter know of her mother's life?
The depths and dangers of those waters,
how she gave birth but did not cling
to motherhood as the only masthead.

What can a daughter know of her mother's hopes?
The hours she spent building her own vessel,
under the moonlight's whittled edges.

I kept the arrows she gave me on my back,
in a quiver, unnamed for years.

I was so sure that nothing could be learned
from the woman at the helm
who considered abandoning ship,
yet never did.

How unoriginal my mutiny
trying to be nothing like her.

How different our arrows,
hers named love, mine regret.

My Father's Dreams

The heat hugged the sidewalks and the orange plastic chairs squeaked under us. Our legs dangled over the edges, not quite reaching the floor. The smell of gasoline that always came home on my dad's shirt hung in the air as we waited and munched on Milky Way bars. We each had a textbook out, mine on the chair beside me, my sister's on her lap, the jackets made of brown paper bag decorated with crayon.

When a car drove up to the pump, a bell would ding twice and my dad would stride his wiry body out, wiping the grease off his hands with a shop towel. We watched as he slid the hose in the tank and the numbers flipped too fast for us to read. His dark hair gleaming, he leaned over the hood of the car, flung the wipers up, and dragged the squeegee in horizontal lines over the windshield, blue drops flying with the flick of his wrist.

Later at home, his hands scrubbed until the grease was just a memory, we waited to wrestle the strongest man we knew. Each of us locked our arms around a bicep and like a mountain he rose as we laughed, our legs hanging in the air. He would roar and pretend to flail, this young father, whose dreams were taking root inside of him.

The Long Drive
—for my parents

A skinny, flask in boot, eighteen-year-old boy,
gunned the gold Mustang convertible
with the engine he rebuilt himself.

She slid into the seat, in her yellow mini skirt
checked her lipstick, felt like royalty
crossing the river out of Kentucky
over the suspension bridge, becoming

the girl no one knew, flinging bits of the legacy
she scorned like confetti from her hands
to flutter into the muddy water below.

The hum of the tires drowned out the taunts,
her mother's wet eyes and horoscope clippings,
her father's silence, her sisters fighting.

One hand tucked in his the other catching the clouds,
wind on her cheekbones, hair blowing
covering her wide smile. He forgot the street
fights, his mom's worry lines,
scraping change together, grease
popping in a hot skillet.

He'll ask twice, she'll swear it's the whiskey.
Not sure she loves him yet, but she knows
she'll go anywhere he asks.

Fifty years later, driving windows down,
Kentucky roads, night songs of crickets
kudzu-covered hills fade into highways.

His lips brushing her knuckles,
her hand now as familiar as his own.

Bisbee Blue

What's she thinking at that moment? My sister's blue eyes
so like mine stare into the camera. She stands on the curved
sidewalk with a desert mountain, dry with scruffy green spots,

covering the sky behind her. I drove from New Mexico burning
my breaks on the switchbacks of the White Mountains,
through the Apache reservation to meet her in the desert.

That day we hiked into mile-high air to the hill crowned
with shrines, little grottos for the holy cut into the rock,
where visitors leave statues, candles, and flowers.

She wears a denim shirt, bag slung over her shoulder,
hint of a serene smile covering her crooked tooth.
A photograph, a shrine, one I didn't realize I was building.

Is a part of us still there? Wearing Bisbee Blue turquoise on our
wrists, driving past the copper mines, deep red bowls scooped
out of the earth, back when everything felt like
the beginning of a story.

Possibly Love

I forget to grind my teeth as I sleep. Instead I dream that I live underwater, in a room wallpapered with green waves–my blood pumps with the rhythm of the tides.

At school, the student who threatened to jump, now wears a parachute, his arm tattooed in his mother tongue, a word he swears means night— or maybe anger—or possibly love.

Last month brought cyclones, those who we thought were too young to die are gone. I dream sand pours into my ears, but my mouth remains empty. I have no language left for this.

When I speak to my father, his voice travels through the phone as if through hallways of loss. I hear the wind buffeting gravestones in a field in Indiana, whistling through valleys in Kentucky.

I imagine him and my mother on the porch of their little house. He sips his coffee as he reads the letter I have yet to write, where I tell him about how time shredded my convictions, about the years that were cyclones upending pieces of my life, rearranging them until I named that rubble holy because I was yanked back to truth there.

After Some Time

The first half of our life is spent being horrified
by our ancestors, tugging the threads out of the loom
of our inheritance, renouncing our parents.

An open wound is a parched throat.
Speaking is like weaving a new thread
a lifeline to pull love back in.

It is possible to make a mosaic from what broke apart,
left fragments behind. Pieces become smooth over time.
Blood red settles, darkness looks lighter in retrospect.

We build bridges to find each other,
realizing what we believed about ourselves
was wrong. No one is beyond repair.

Field Guide to Forgiveness

I lock my journals in my desk in case I die out there.
I don't want anyone to know that I sometimes wish
I had a daughter, someone to see the ways
I've sacrificed. Someone to tell me how I've failed.

I walk naked into the desert until my body
becomes sand. My hair, a halo of crows.
I know which part to sever first.
Was it always going to be that I was the last one I'd forgive?

I set up camp in the crumbling landscape.
There is no God here. Just me, the wind, the rattlesnakes.
I'll see this through. I'll take that bitter meat from my chest,
fling it into the desert. Feed the wolves this one last time.

bruises & lies

That Boy

Once the kids at my new school
saw I got off the bus on Vine Street,
everything changed.

You can't step off the bus
into a sidewalk of hookers,
dealers, and pimps and still expect
people to see the you
they saw before.

Every day on the bus
he turned his head to smile
over the top of green seat backs
until eventually he sat beside me.

He didn't care about Vine Street
even though he lived in the suburbs.
Sandy-haired and blue-eyed he wore jerseys,
rode his bike on tree-lined streets,
had friends who looked like him.

I leaned against the bus window,
with each bump my head
bounced against the glass.

He slipped his baseball mitt
under my head, a pillow.
He said, *sleep, I'll wake you up.*
It smelled like dirt, leather, him.

After School

When my stepdaughters tell stories
of lacrosse games, recitals,
who was more flexible,
who danced in Swan Lake,

I listen but don't speak
because after my school days,
I ran home
my sister ahead of me
her black-heeled shoes flying
leading the way
pushing so hard up the steep hill,
she'd get migraines
by the time she fell on the carpet
right inside
the front door.

As we ran the rocks came
hurled with curses,
Run white girls run.

It was a game
no one ever won.

Hail Mary

When I remember fear,
it's not a ghoul in the closet.
It's a leer in the dark,
a girl and how she lost it.

Don't go there, that street is scary,
Four Our Fathers, One Hail Mary.

Shave the darkness down,
into small pieces to ignore.
Forget sinister clowns,
a man's been shot dead next door.

Don't go there, that alley is scary,
Four Our Fathers, One Hail Mary.

Lock fear in a soft room,
dead man jumped over the moon.
I asked the nun what's a sin.
She drew a circle filled it in.

Hail Mary full of grace,
Wipe that smile from your face.

Red Rover Red Rover
call the father, the holy ghost,
send someone over,
Pandora's been dosed,

Hail Mary full of grace,
Wipe that smile from your face.

In the dark, my soul to keep,
Mother may I go to sleep?
Fear was my original sin.
it is what would do me in.

Thirteen in the 80's

Hard to say how it all got started
when I moved to the country
from the city, I learned about
cow tipping and mudding. I learned
about big quiet nights and cornfields.
He gave me cinnamon gum
on the school bus and later
we learned how to smoke weed
using a can, a potato, aluminum foil.

On T.V. they were trying to scare us
by frying eggs—*This is your brain on drugs.*
We'd take a drag and laugh, then watch
another *After School Special*, where we learned
men driving vans are definitely dangerous,
alcoholics hide vodka bottles in closets,
and teens carry their problems in backpacks
that adults never see through.

Hard to say what came first
sips of Boones Farm Strawberry Hill,
warm Miller Lite, singing the lyrics
to "Pour Some Sugar on Me."
He wasn't mine. I pushed him away
after he held me too close on the dance floor
his heart thundering in his chest.
My first kiss, someone else.

Hard to say how it happened
wearing ripped jeans, smoking Marlboros,
watching reruns of *Happy Days*
on his couch, then later, without him,
trying on bohemian, cynic, nomad, not noticing
or caring about the way my feet slipped,
the way I always returned like a boomerang
wanting that first taste.

Just Another Girl

In my college classes
I looked like them,
but underneath fault lines rattled.

In crowded hallways
I rounded my shoulders
slithered passed, jaw clenched
eyes forward, my body
an asylum for old wounds.

My roommates didn't know
I slept with a knife under my pillow,
kept my black boots unlaced at the side of my bed
looked for the windows and all the ways out.

One night during a party at our house
a guy pulled out a gun, showing off, pointing it.
I was the only one to tell him
get the hell out.

Then they knew I was different.
They said I wasn't scared
but they were wrong.

I carried a knife at all times,
one I would never use.
On those campus streets
I was two people,
blurring the line
between languages
for who I was,
and who I might become.

vows & ghosts

An Almost Honeymoon

Riding through the salty air of Cape Cod
on trails dappled with sun,

it was easy to forget the house
we'd be returning to in New York.

Easy to forget we were unaccustomed
to spending weekdays together,

and folding laundry, falling asleep
or struggling to sleep, and yet these

were our lessons to learn like newlyweds
returning from a honeymoon,

but I wasn't wearing a ring yet and
he'd already had his children.

Pine needles softened the terrain
their clean smell washed over us,

but I could not shake the feeling
that no amount of my pictures on the walls

or shoes laying by the door could
compare to the life he lived before me.

Befriending the Ghost

I wish I'd never let her in. Curse
my polite Midwestern smile

that I can't seem to scrub away
with the Northeastern wind.

I try to shake her off like a bad habit
but she's crossed over, won't leave

crashing my middle-aged marriage.
Just when I'm ready to tell her

she's outstayed her welcome
she quotes a line from Rilke

the one about terrifying angels,
reminding me she's slumming it here,

roaming in soft slippers, crunching
Pringles in my ear, binge watching Netflix,

she remains like a zipper stuck,
a corset of bone that pinches.

What a Day Can Mean

Tomorrow is Valentine's Day,
the day to condense love
into the folds of a card.
I heard there is an app showing
which bars in NYC are giving
free condoms for the night.
Maybe with enough luck and alcohol
sex can equal love.

I had a dream I sold houses.
Inside of each, movies projected
on the empty walls.
Memories without color—
memories of how love left.

We are planning a June wedding,
on the Hudson's bronze cliffs.
Before we both say *I do,*
we will cast our regrets in the river,
let the tide take them where tides go—
into the estuary, into the bays,
under the barges, beneath bridges.

By then, the ice and freezing air
will have melted away.
We won't remember
how cold we are now.
We never do.

Rope Burns

I only hid in the bathroom once.
The entire weekend
felt like a boat pitching back and forth.

Each time we visited my mother-in-law
at the memory care facility,
she called me his ex-wife's name,
her first daughter-in-law.

When the forgetting starts
it's the little things—
Did I go to the bank?
Then the dangerous things—
How do I get home?
In the end, years are erased as easily as minutes.

Each time we laughed, told her my name
until we finally stopped. My stepdaughters
said it's no big deal. My husband said that too.

I am not petty, but I am clutching
the rope connecting her to me,
to my memories of loving her.
My arms are shaking, my hands raw.

Everything
    —a love poem for H.S.

Long time
since I
was bruised
on purpose,

still
I flinch
when you
reach too quickly.

I brought calluses,
one part hope
two parts shame
refusal to ever quit.
Blame the coal miners
I come from
stubborn,
not afraid
of the dark.

Your imperfections
were needed.
If you were too good,
I would have
turned from you.
No one wants a saint,
no one wants
to hide their sweet flinches,
scars all the time.

Your embrace
the solid ground
I craved.
Your hand in mine
everything.

Let's stand here
and fight
those junkyard dogs
together.

bullets & seeds

Planning for the End of the World

Let's darken the windows
with a No. 2 pencil, pretend
danger isn't a white boy with rage.

Let's push the desks against the door
then analyze whether
love or death drove Ophelia mad.

Let's remain vigilant but human
enough to let ourselves
feel haunted—feel hunted
by our conscience
as we ask children to
support arguments with evidence
look for facts from credible sources
but never shed a tear or drop
of blue or black ink.

Slip a gun
in my hand
instead of chalk?
Since you asked—
Yes, I will die
for your children
when the time comes.

Decades from now,
what story will the history books tell
about how our children ducked
into closets, huddled in corners?

Hush
          hold still
don't talk
away from the windows
          lights out

ashes ashes

we all fall down.

A Citizen

The next time you stop speaking,
ask yourself why you were born.
        —Naomi Shihab Nye, *"Separation Wall"*

When you peel an orange
it is still whole, only more vulnerable.   .

The next time you can't cry
ask yourself how you survived

or why you still persist when loss
sings an anthem pointing a gun.

Pretend opioids are scared of skin
AR-15s frightened of lunch boxes
pretend tear gas is afraid of violins.

When I bite into a ripe strawberry
my mouth full of seeds and juice,

I want to feel like a citizen
of a country that protects us all,

where a Black man kneeling
is the same as a white man kneeling,

where a white man kneeling won't mean
a Black man can't breathe.

I want to be able to tell the children
I teach, no matter who you are
in this land, you will survive.

The Day I Heard,

we reached 60 thousand deaths,
I noticed the slumbering
rosebush in the yard

had become a tumbleweed
of thorns, brittle sticks
and blackened buds,
where life had trickled out.

With my pruners in hand,
I separated branches,
thrust my body forward
welcoming the sting
of the thorn on skin
through my sleeves,
pinpricks through my gloves,
a drum roll of small fires
snagging my skin as I dove in.

Later in the tub, my cuts stinging
under warm water. I ran my finger
over a puncture, the shape
of a checkmark or a wing
on the soft part of my belly.

I thought about a girl I knew
who cut herself—those tightropes of scars
on her arms and legs—
a banner, a release
because sometimes crying isn't enough
and pain is proof, however temporary,
that she still stood.

I felt no need to offer an apology,
I knew the roses would return by July,
brash pink shouts of summer
when our grief is tenfold.

A Promise or a Prayer

Dogwood blooms will breach the sky again,
under the decaying bough green shoots rise.

Whatever we have lost,
because we have all lost something,
will leave a field open within us.

New life, grafted from all we've borne,
will grow, though we may never see it.

All the ways I've been at war with the world
and myself are done now,
the reasons forgotten.

If there is anyone to forgive,
Do it now, I tell myself.

I think it may be a sin
not to love during these times.

Embrace

When the hand you reach for is gone,
you are a leaf curling into itself
stunned by frost.

A bloom closing nighttime
in its throat only to bare
its darkness to each sunrise.

Animal of your own heart,
home in the shelter of your skin.

The inevitable truth of being human
is that everything you love will fail you
at one time or another.

Cradle the wing split by shame,
name the tributaries of loss,
bless the lessons life etched onto you.

Be brave enough to open the door
when your heart,
that beggar in rags, knocks.

Scared, imperfect, broken
gather the pieces
and love them anyway.

mirrors & roads

Recipe for Losing Oneself

a slow cooked meal
make sure you have the necessary ingredients before you start

> ½ pound of rejection
> *can be substituted with parental absence, collective*
> *trauma, or inherited dysfunction*

> 6 ounces of shame
> *may have a bitter taste if it comes from addiction or*
> *poverty*

> 2 cups of isolation
> *leave or be left, you were meant to be alone*

> 1 cup of betrayal
> *can substitute guilt (a smokier flavor if you were the one*
> *who did it)*

> 1 tablespoon of fear
> *just one memory of violence but must leave lasting echoes*
> *in your skin twenty years later*

> two teaspoons of degradation
> *sex, preferably while drunk, must be indiscriminate, using*
> *the body as a weapon or a doorway*

Preheat the oven to *it must be this hot in hell.*

Marinate for at least 10 years. Bake until hardened on the outside but
still tender in the middle.

Recipe serves one

How to Deal with Aging

Look at old photos of yourself regularly.
Remember how you hid
in your smooth face and body.
You were learning appropriateness from rednecks,
nuns, and absent parents.

Your vowels were elongated, hair teased high,
the questions no one answered
you tucked under your shirt
like the door key around your neck.
They taught you to type, say the Hail Mary
then sent you on your way.

Remember the arithmetic of secrets.
Remember when you kissed
the red-haired boy hard
pressing lips to teeth,
leaving bruises on each other's necks,
long before you understood you were
expected to be both pliant and tough.

Look in the mirror regularly
without makeup,
without wincing,

then look again with the lights out.
You see yourself clearly now.

Birthright

The women I came from crawled
under a sky that would never be theirs
stealing crumbs of light yearning for more.

They told me not to fling the window open
searching the night skies for the missing pieces of myself.
They told me a woman eats her sins,
and swallows the pain of others.

My mother buried weapons under her tongue
to work in a man's world.

My grandmother, an artist, had eleven children, lost five more.
She picked up her paintbrush again right before she died,

My great grandmother, whose long hair reached the floor,
cut it all off to defy the husband who loved it.

They began the story that I will finish.
There is a woman inside me
I was always destined to become.
My ancestors knew:
their palms pounded out
the only revolution my blood has ever known.

Why is it that when a woman lights herself on fire
it is mistaken for sacrifice or love
rather than the truth she was born to tell?

A Strong Fate

I drove down the same streets that were flooded yesterday,
saw a man sitting like Buddha in the middle of the sidewalk
his bags gathered like disciples around him.
I read about another man whose dreams told
him to build an ark. On faith, he listened.

I have almost died twice, once at the moment I was born
once at the moment I was saved. What happened in between
left me for dead too. Because I lived, someone once
told me I had a strong fate. I wish he would have said *faith*
but I doubt it's true.

After floods, it's easier to cry. *Let go*, my heart says.
Because the smell of lilacs —piercing and flawless,
because the summer sky stretching in its hopeful
expansiveness. Because the ache toward
forgiveness has begun to outweigh the deed.

Directions to Your Lost Self

Your GPS won't work on this journey, no signal. Tattoo the coordinates on your palm of where and when you left yourself— you were five years old and you fled your body, you were twenty-five and numb.

Let those blue numbers unravel, become the ropes you grasp like a woman climbing up to an ancient city in the cliffs, where she can exchange currencies: experience for sustenance, her sorrows for strength.

1. Get on the main road, drive until the wheat fields look like hands waving, until the land blurs.

2. At the boulder shaped like a man eating his knees, turn right onto the highway.

3. Merge. Don't pay attention to the signs only the mile markers inside you.

With each mile you breathe deeper. Now the memories come. Let each spread like a drop of ink on water.

4. The last bit of road is the trickiest—hairpin curves, high winds, rockslides, animal crossings, but do whatever it takes—ride horseback or camel, walk or crawl.

5. When you get to the top, rest. You'll recognize where you are. You once thought you came here to die but really it was to surrender.

She's still here, search among the unmarked stones, dig until you find her. Pull that sweet girl out of the mud and moss, embrace her. Thank her for living even when covered, thank her for never losing hope that you'd eventually return to yourself.

Rebecca Watkins, an educator and poet, earned her M.F.A. in Poetry and her M.S. Ed from the City University of New York. Besides being a teacher, she has created and led poetry workshops for all ages in the Hudson Valley. In 2015, she was awarded a writing residency in Honduras and taught poetry at an orphanage and bilingual school. She was a contributing poetry editor of River River Literary Journal until 2020. Rebecca has been published in *Sin Fronteras, New Feather's Anthology, Roanoke Review, The Red Mesa Review, Anderbo,* and *the SNReview* among other literary journals. Her first full-length poetry book *Sometimes, in These Places* was published by Unsolicited Press in 2017. More of her work can be found at *www. rebeccawatkinswriter.com.*

www.ingramcontent.com/pod-product-compliance
Lightning Source LLC
Chambersburg PA
CBHW020225090426
42734CB00008B/1213